CCSS **Genre** Expository

Essential Question

What makes different parts of the world different?

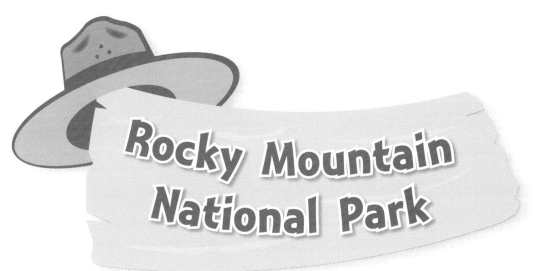

Rocky Mountain National Park

by Betsy Hebert

How Is the Park Special?

The Rocky Mountains are big.

Have you been to the Rocky Mountains? People call them the Rockies.

The Rockies start in Alaska. They end in New Mexico. That's a long way!

KEY
- Rocky Mountains
- ★ Rocky Mountain National Park
- United States
- Water

Canada

Rocky
★ Mountain
National Park

Pacific
Ocean

Mexico

Rocky Mountain **National** Park is a special place. Can you find it on the map?

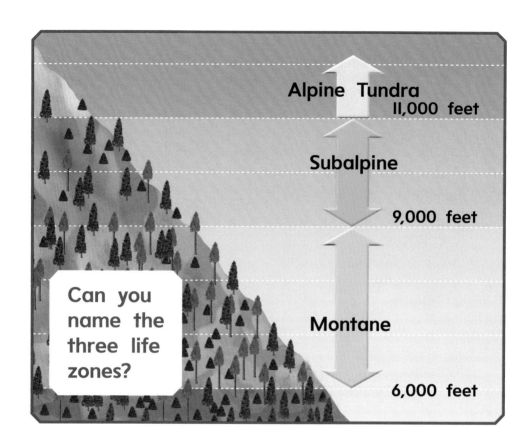

The park has three life **zones**.

Each zone has different plants and animals. Each zone has a different climate.

STOP AND CHECK

How many life zones does the park have?

4

What Is the Montane?

Pine trees grow in this zone.

Let's look at the lowest zone. This **location** is the montane.

It starts at 6,000 feet. It goes up to 9,000 feet.

These are aspen trees.

The montane is the warmest zone. Tall pine trees grow here. Aspen trees do too. Flowers grow in **meadows**.

Squirrels like pine nuts.

Many animals can live here. Squirrels eat seeds. Elk eat grass. Bobcats hunt. Bluebirds and jays nest.

STOP AND CHECK

What is the montane zone like?

What Is the Subalpine?

Spruce trees grow here.

The subalpine is the middle zone. It starts at 9,000 feet. It goes up to 11,000 feet.

It rains more here. It is mostly dark **forests**.

These trees live
hundreds of years.

The forest is thinner here.
Twisted trees grow at the top
of this zone.

Cold winds **bend** the trees.
The wind changes their **growth**.

Pine martens
have thick fur.

Who lives here? Mule deer find food in the warm **seasons**. Pine martens like it here. Juncos and chickadees make nests.

STOP AND CHECK

What is the subalpine zone like?

What Is the Alpine Tundra?

The alpine tundra is the highest zone. It starts at 11,000 feet. The ground is always **frozen**.

Some flowers bloom in spring.

It snows a lot. There are no trees.

But some plants grow here. They are small and low. They stay out of the strong winds.

12

Pikas are small and furry.

This is a bighorn sheep.

Only a few animals live here.
Bighorn sheep climb over rocks.
Pikas make **dens**.

Now you have seen the three
life zones.

People hike in the park.

Rocky Mountain National Park is a special place!

STOP AND CHECK

What is the alpine tundra zone like?

Respond to Reading

Summarize

What is *Rocky Mountain National Park* about? The chart may help you.

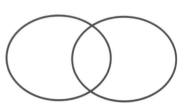

Text Evidence

1. Compare the montane and the alpine tundra zones. Compare and Contrast

2. Which is the *middle* zone? What is another way of saying *middle*? Vocabulary

3. Write about the plants in each zone. Write About Reading

Compare Texts

What makes Yellowstone a special part of the Rocky Mountains?

Yellowstone

Yellowstone is in the Rockies.
It is special, too.

This park has hot springs.

Geysers

Some hot springs shoot water into the air. These are called geysers.

Rob Steffin/The Image Bank/Getty Images

Mudpots

Mudpots are hot springs, too. Hot steam comes up through **layers** of mud. It makes bubbles.

Make Connections
How is Yellowstone special?
Essential Question

Would you rather visit Yellowstone National Park or Rocky Mountain National Park? Explain. Text to Text

Focus on Science

Purpose To find out more about Rocky Mountain National Park or Yellowstone

---

What to Do

Step 1 ➤ Work with a partner. Choose one national park you liked in this book.

Step 2 ➤ Make a poster about the national park.

Conclusion Tell why you chose the park. What makes it special?